Little Science Stars

GW00729858

What Things Are Made Of

The Best Start in Science

By Helen Orme

ticktock

ISBN-13: 978 1 84898 062 4 pbk
This revised edition published in 2009 by *ticktock* Media Ltd

Printed in China
9 8 7 6 5 4 3 2 1

Copyright © *ticktock* Entertainment Ltd 2005

First published in Great Britain as *Check It Out!* in 2005 by *ticktock* Media Ltd, The Old Sawmill, 103 Goods Station Road, Tunbridge Wells, Kent, TN1 2DP

Picture credits (t=top, b=bottom, c=centre, l=left, r=right, OFC=outside front cover, OBC=outside back cover):

Corbis 13tl, 13bl, 14 all. Fancy/Veer/Corbis: OFCbl. Photodisc: 6t, 9t, 18t. Powerstock: 10b, 15tr. Shutterstock: OFCt, 1 all, 2, 3 all, 4–5 all, 6c, 6b, 7 all, 8 all, 9c, 9b, 10t, 10c,11 all, 12 all, 13r, 13cl, 14–15, 15t, 15b (both), 16 all, 17 all, 18b, 19 all, 20 all, 21 all, 22–23 all, 24t, OBC both.

Every effort has been made to trace the copyright holders and we apologize in advance for any unintentional omissions. We would be pleased to insert the appropriate acknowledgements in any subsequent edition of this publication.

Contents

Any words appearing in the text in bold, **like this**,
are explained in the Glossary.

Look at all the things around you. Have you ever wondered what they are made of?

Metal

Cotton plant

Trees

Look at the pictures of the fizzy drinks cans, the boys' colourful T-shirts and the books.

Now look at the pictures of the **metal**, cotton plant and trees.

Can you match these things with the **material** they are made from?

What are materials?

All the things around us are made of materials. We use different materials to make different objects.

Metal, **plastic, cloth, glass, paper** and **wood** are some of the materials that we use every day.

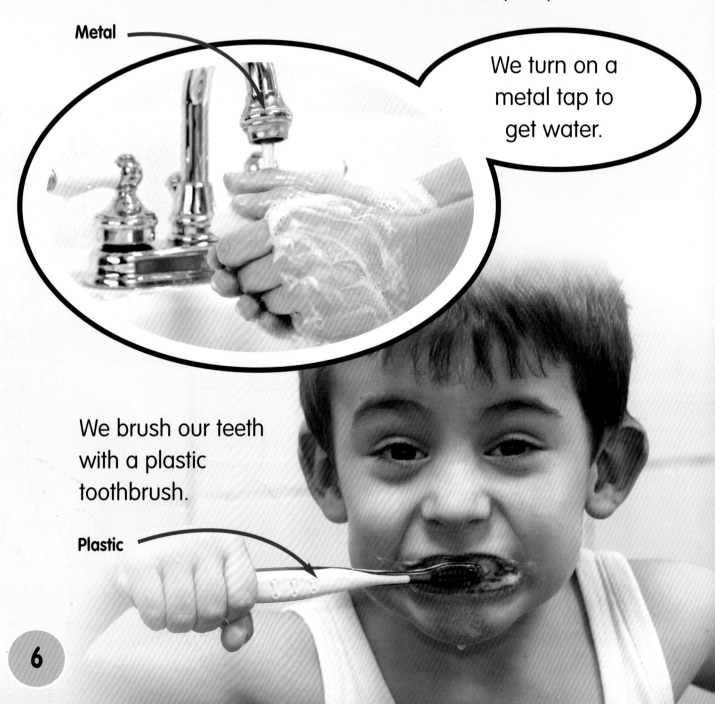

Metal

We turn on a metal tap to get water.

We brush our teeth with a plastic toothbrush.

Plastic

Our clothes are made from cloth
– come on, get dressed!

Cloth

Grown-ups like
to read the
newspaper.

Paper

We drink orange
juice from a glass.

Glass

Wood

Open the front
door – time for
school!

Where does stone come from?

Stone is a hard, heavy **natural** material. Mountains and cliffs are made of stone.

Mountains

Stone is dug out of the ground and from the sides of cliffs and mountains using diggers.

Digger

Stone does not bend, but it can be broken into pieces.

Rough stones

Smooth stones

8

Stone can be cut into shapes.

These huge stone faces have been cut into the side of a mountain in America.

Stone pyramid – 4,500 years old

Many buildings are made from stone.

Stone lasts a long time.

Stone castle – 600 years old

What is metal?

Metal is a material made from some types of stone.

Stone that contains metal is called ore.

The ore is smashed into powder. Then the powder is heated so the metal comes out of the stone.

Iron ore

Copper ore

Metals are hard like stone, but they will bend.

Metal is a good material for making things like bendy fence wire.

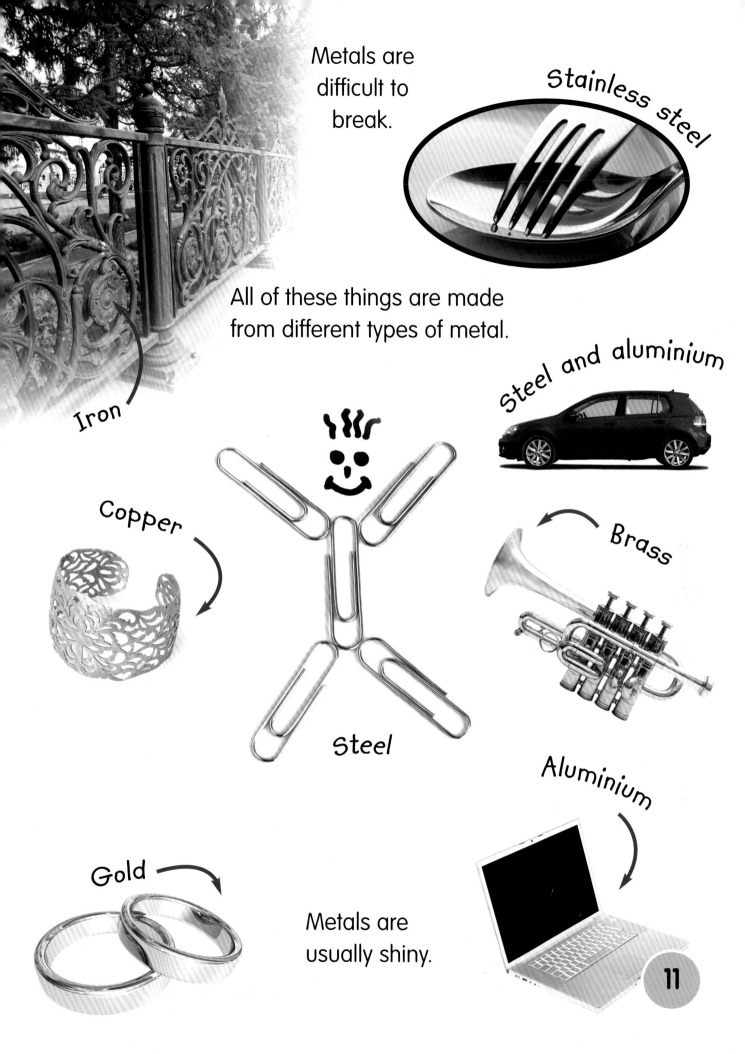

Metals are difficult to break.

Stainless steel

All of these things are made from different types of metal.

Iron

Steel and aluminium

Copper

Brass

Steel

Aluminium

Gold

Metals are usually shiny.

11

Where does wood come from?

Wood is a natural material. It comes from trees.

Wood

Trees

The trees are cut down using a chainsaw.

Chainsaw

The wood is taken to a factory called a sawmill.

The wood is cut and shaped with metal tools.

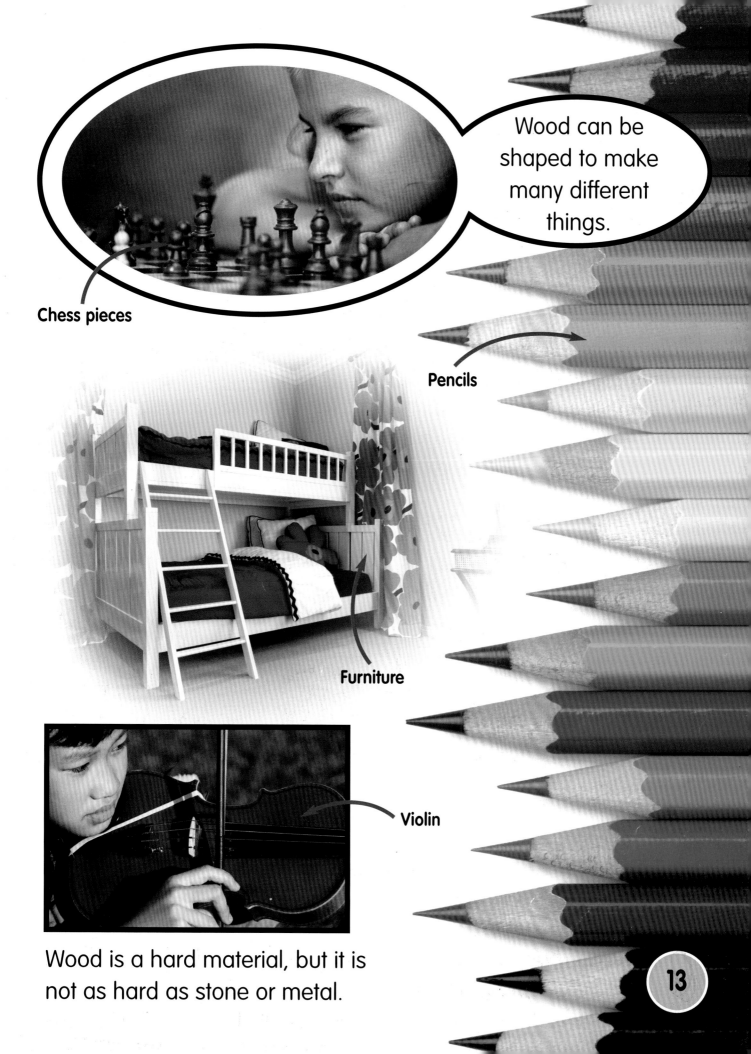

Wood can be shaped to make many different things.

Chess pieces

Pencils

Furniture

Violin

Wood is a hard material, but it is not as hard as stone or metal.

13

What is paper made from?

Paper is a soft **artificial** material that
is made from wood.

Pulp

The wood is
chopped into tiny pieces.
Then it is soaked in water
to make a mushy mixture
called **pulp**.

The pulp is then
squeezed out
into thin sheets
and dried.

You cannot fold or bend
wood, but you can bend
and fold paper.

You can sit on a chair made from wood...

...but a paper chair would not be very strong!

We use paper in lots of different ways!

Books

Note pad

Wrapping paper

How is glass made?

Glass is a hard artificial material.
It is made from sand.

The sand is heated
until it is very, very hot.

The sand melts and
turns into glass.

Hot, soft glass

Hot glass is soft. It can be
made into different shapes
before it cools down and
becomes hard.

Glass is **transparent**. This means that light can pass through it.

Glass windows let light in and allow us to see out.

Clear glass bowl

We can see what's inside a glass container.

Don't touch broken glass!

The edges of broken glass will cut you.

What is plastic made from?

Plastic is an artificial material. It is made from **crude oil**. We find oil under the ground.

This machine is pumping oil from under the ground.

The oil is sent to a **refinery**.

At the refinery, the oil is heated to produce plastic and other useful substances such as petrol.

Refinery

Plastic can be made in any shape and colour.

Plastic can be bendy...

...or hard

...or soft.

Plastic bottle

Plastic bag

Plastic can also be transparent – you can see through it!

19

What is cloth made from?

Cloth is an artificial material made from **fibres**.

Natural fibres

Plastic fibres

Some cloth is made from plastic fibres. Some cloth is made from natural fibres.

Woollen cloth is made of natural fibres from sheep.

Cotton cloth is made of natural fibres from the cotton plant.

The fibres are spun into a continuous **yarn**.

Then the yarn is made into cloth.

Cloth is a very soft material.

It can easily be folded.

Cloth is made into many things such as T-shirts, jeans and jumpers.

Questions and answers

Q Look around your bedroom. How many things can you find made from metal, wood, paper, plastic and cloth?

A Here are some ideas to get you started:
Pyjamas – cloth
Comics – paper
Trainers – plastic

Q What is the pattern in wood called?

A It is called the "grain".

Q What can we do with used paper?

A We can recycle it! Used paper can be turned back into pulp and made into new paper.

Q Which animals can we get wool from?

A We can get wool from sheep, goats, alpacas and llamas.

Alpaca

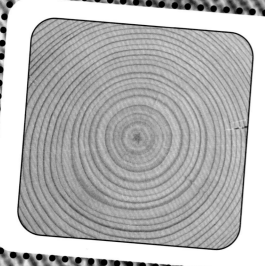

Q How can you work out the age of a tree?

A A tree grows a new ring inside its trunk each year. You can find out the age of the tree by counting the rings.

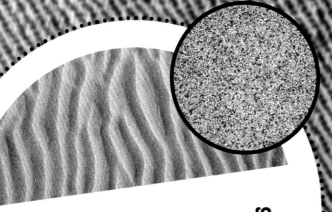

Q What is sand made of?

A Sand is made of millions of tiny pieces of stone.

Q What two materials is this hammer made of?

A Metal and wood.

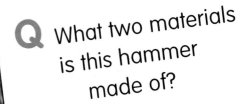

Glossary

Artificial Describes anything that is made by people.

Cloth A type of material that is made from fibres which have been joined together by weaving or knitting.

Crude oil Oil that has been pumped from under the ground. It is natural and has not had anything done to it by people.

Fibres Long, thin pieces of plastic, cotton or wool.

Glass A transparent material made from sand.

Material Any substance that things are made from.

Metal A hard, strong material such as gold or steel.

Natural Describes anything that is made by nature.

Paper A lightweight material made from wood.

Plastic An artificial material made from crude oil. It can be made into almost anything!

Pulp A mixture that is wet and mushy.

Refinery A large factory where crude oil is taken to be made into things such as petrol and plastic.

Stone A hard, heavy natural material that can be dug from cliffs or mountains and used to make buildings.

Transparent When something is see-through and allows light to pass through it.

Wood A natural material that comes from trees.

Yarn A long thread made from fibres that have been twisted together.

Index